A SOLDIER'S LIFE IN
VICTORIAN TIMES

C555077793

A SOLDIER'S LIFE IN
VICTORIAN TIMES

Fiona Corbridge

FRANKLIN WATTS
LONDON • SYDNEY

Illustrations by
Mark Bergin
Kevin Maddison
Lee Montgomery
Nick Spender
Peter Visscher
Mike White
Maps by Stefan Chabluk

This edition 2009

First published in 2006 by Franklin Watts

Copyright © Franklin Watts 2006

Franklin Watts
338 Euston Road
London NW1 3BH

Franklin Watts Australia
Hachette Children's Books
Level 17/207 Kent Street
Sydney NSW 2000

All rights reserved.

A CIP catalogue record
for this book is available
from the British Library.

Dewey number: 355.00941

ISBN 978 0 7496 8872 1

Printed in China

Franklin Watts is a division of Hachette
Children's Books, an Hachette Livre UK
company. www.hachettelivre.co.uk

This book is based on
Going to War in Victorian Times
by Craig Dodd © Franklin Watts 2000.
It is produced for Franklin Watts
by Painted Fish Ltd.
Designer: Rita Storey

Series editor: John C. Miles
Art director: Jonathan Hair

CONTENTS

THE WORLD 1850–80

During the nineteenth century, soldiers were at war all over the world, especially in 1850–80.

Armies fought each other in Europe, the Balkans, India, Africa, the USA and the Far East. Thousands of men died in the fighting. Many thousands more died later of their wounds or from diseases caught in army camps and hospitals.

UNION STATES OF AMERICA

American Civil War

CONFEDERATE STATES OF AMERICA

Abraham Lincoln (1809–65)
Abraham Lincoln was the US president during the American Civil War. He led the Union states to win, but was shot dead by John Wilkes Booth.

War in the Crimea, 1854

War broke out in the Crimea in Russia when the Russians decided to take over Ottoman (Turkish) land. France and Britain fought Russia to stop the Russians getting a way through to the Mediterranean Sea.

Mutiny in India, 1857

Indian soldiers who worked for the British East India Company were given bullets greased with cow and pig fat. This was against their religion. The soldiers had a mutiny which lasted for over a year.

Otto von Bismarck (1815–98)
Bismarck was the head of the government in the German state of Prussia. He built up his country's army and got the many German states to join together into one powerful nation.

RUSSIA

Crimean War

BRITAIN

PRUSSIA

FRANCE

Franco-Prussian War

MEDITERRANEAN SEA

OTTOMAN EMPIRE

ATLANTIC OCEAN

INDIA

Indian Mutiny

INDIAN OCEAN

WORLD MAP 1850–80

Wars and fighting

Queen Victoria (1819–1901)
Victoria became queen of Britain in 1837. "Victorian times" means "during Victoria's rule". Britain managed to build a huge empire in these years.

The American Civil War, 1860

America was made up of states under a central government. The southern states (Confederates) broke away from the northern states (the Union). This started the American Civil War (US Civil War).

The Franco-Prussian War, 1870–71

The German state of Prussia went to war with France. After eight months, the French surrendered (gave up and agreed Prussia had won). Germany was now the most powerful country in mainland Europe.

JOINING THE ARMY

Some soldiers were volunteers – they decided to join the army. Others were conscripts – the government made them join. Conscripts served in the army for a fixed time before going back to their ordinary jobs. They could be called up to fight for their country at any time.

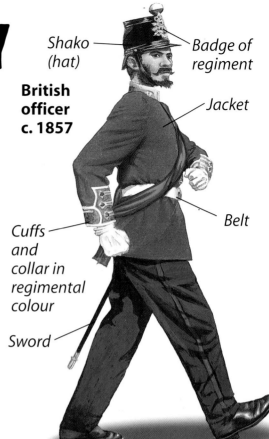

British officer c. 1857

Shako (hat)

Badge of regiment

Jacket

Belt

Cuffs and collar in regimental colour

Sword

ARMY OFFICERS

Being an officer was a good career. In Britain, a rich family could buy their son a job as an officer.

Things were different in the USA. In the US Civil War, some groups of soldiers voted for their own officers.

REGIMENTS

In the nineteenth century, armies were organized into large groups of men called regiments.

The British army had regiments from different parts of the country.

Their names showed where they came from, for example the Lincolnshire Regiment.

Army recruiting sergeants sometimes visited village pubs to talk to young men and try to get them to join the army.

Regimental badge

CONSCRIPTS IN EUROPE

Prussia

In the 1860s, Bismarck (the ruler of Prussia) decided that all young men had to do military service. By the 1870s, Prussia had more than 700,000 conscripts who were trained and ready to fight.

France

France had a different system. Every man was given a number. If his number was chosen, he had to become a conscript for up to seven years. Some men paid someone else to take their place.

French soldier c. 1860

Prussian soldier c. 1870

Wide-brimmed hat

Musket (gun)

Blanket roll (for sleeping)

Water canteen (water bottle)

US Confederate conscript, 1862

AMERICA

Before the US Civil War, each state had a militia. Militiamen were part-time soldiers who met to practise fighting so that if a war began, they would be ready to fight.

AMERICAN CIVIL WAR

The two sides in the US Civil War were the Union and the Confederates.

Most soldiers were volunteers, but the Confederates started conscription in 1862. Union states had rules saying how many soldiers each state had to recruit.

COMMANDERS

The ruler of a country is often the head of the armed forces. In the USA, the president is the commander-in-chief of the armed forces.

During the US Civil War, President Abraham Lincoln was very busy commanding the soldiers of the Union states.

A British fusilier

A Union general in the US Civil War

WEST POINT

There is a famous US military academy called West Point. Many senior officers in the US Civil War trained there. They included Ulysses S. Grant, commander of the Union army, and Robert E. Lee, who commanded the Confederate forces.

Grant led the Union army to win and later became president of the USA.

RANKS

Armies are divided up into ranks. Commanders are the top rank and privates are the bottom rank.

Privates are known by a different name in some regiments – fusiliers, gunners, guardsmen or troopers.

(Right) Ulysses S. Grant

RANKS IN THE BRITISH ARMY, 1860

The highest rank was field marshal. Field marshals commanded whole armies.

Below field marshals were generals. Generals planned what the troops would do on the battlefield.

Colonels commanded infantry regiments. Lieutenant-colonels commanded artillery and cavalry regiments.

Majors and captains were in charge of units in each regiment. They were helped by junior officers, such as lieutenants.

The regimental sergeant-major was in charge of discipline (rules and behaviour). Sergeants led small groups of men and made sure officers' orders were obeyed. Next came corporals and lance-corporals.

The lowest rank was the private.

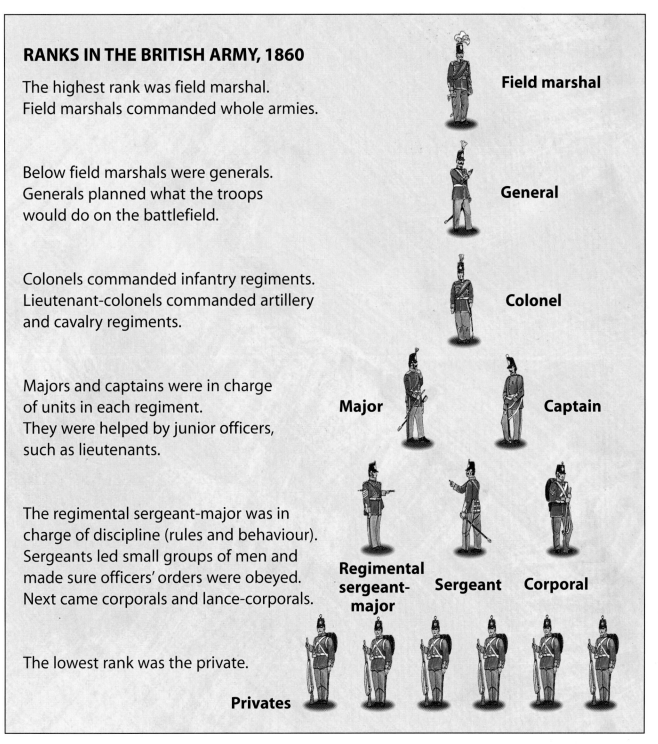

Field marshal

General

Colonel

Major   Captain

Regimental sergeant-major   Sergeant   Corporal

Privates

JOINING A REGIMENT

In the nineteenth century, armies in Europe and the USA were made up of regiments. Infantry regiments fought on foot. Artillery regiments used large mounted guns. Cavalry regiments rode horses.

In Britain, a regiment was usually divided into two. One part worked abroad while the other stayed in Britain.

During the US Civil War, many men joined their local militia. Militia units often became part of a larger regiment. Regiments were on active service (on duty) throughout the war.

UNIFORMS

Union soldier in the US Civil War

Wearing a uniform helped soldiers to act as part of a team. It also made it easier for men to recognize other soldiers in their regiment in battle. That was why each regiment had a slightly different uniform.

Kepi (cap)

Rolled blanket and backpack

Jacket

Cartridge pouch

Belt

Haversac

Tin mug

Musket

Wars and fighting in the nineteenth century

• *Crimean War, 1854. Russia against France and Britain.*

• *Indian Mutiny, 1857. Britain against Indian soldiers.*

• *US Civil War, 1860. Union states against Confederate states.*

• *Franco-Prussian War, 1870. France against Prussia.*

US UNIFORMS

In the US Civil War, Union soldiers wore dark blue jackets with lighter blue trousers. Confederate forces wore grey jackets and blue or brown trousers. Each regiment's uniform was slightly different. But as the war went on and it became hard to get materials, soldiers had to wear uniforms made out of rough brown cloth.

HATS AND HELMETS

France
French soldiers wore a hat called a shako. It was made of leather, with a small peak and a coloured pompom on top.

Prussian helmet

Confederate army kepi

Prussia
Prussian soldiers wore helmets with a spike on top. The French army copied these after it lost the Franco-Prussian War.

Pompom

French shako

America
Most Union soldiers wore a cap with a peak called a kepi. Confederate troops wore a hat with a wide brim, or a kepi with a blue band.

THE COLOUR OF DUST
British troops in India wore lightweight khaki uniforms because it was so hot. The word "khaki" means "dust-coloured" in Urdu (an Indian language). Khaki uniforms merged into the landscape and made soldiers more difficult for an enemy to spot.

British cavalry trooper in a khaki uniform, 1850

Victoria Cross

Medal of Honor

MEDALS FOR BRAVERY
Britain's highest military medal is the Victoria Cross, named after Queen Victoria. The highest military medal in the USA is the Medal of Honor. These medals are given to soldiers who have shown great bravery.

Both medals were introduced between 1850 and 1880.

TOO BRIGHT FOR SAFETY
Soldiers in bright uniforms were easy for the enemy to see and shoot. By 1890, most countries had changed their soldiers' uniforms to duller colours.

INFANTRY

In a battle, the infantry tried to break through the lines of enemy soldiers. In the early 1800s, they fired their guns then charged (rushed forward) at the enemy.

By 1870, armies had guns that were quicker to reload. Soldiers could keep firing and no longer needed to charge at the enemy.

A British infantryman loads his musket (gun)

Ramrod pushes the gunpowder cartridge down the barrel

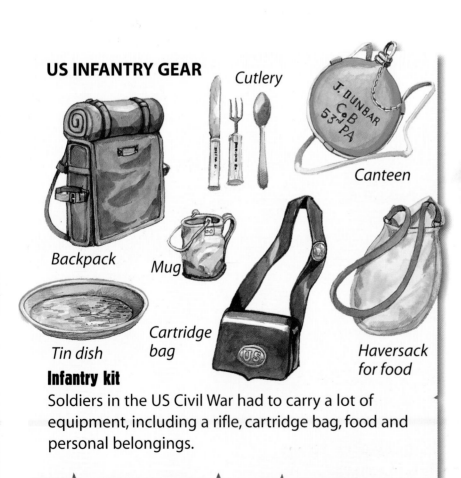

US INFANTRY GEAR

Cutlery

Canteen

J. DUNBAR
C B
53 PA

Backpack

Mug

Tin dish

Cartridge bag

Haversack for food

Infantry kit
Soldiers in the US Civil War had to carry a lot of equipment, including a rifle, cartridge bag, food and personal belongings.

MUZZLE-LOADERS
Guns used in the early 1800s were loaded from the muzzle (front end). The soldier pushed a cartridge containing gunpowder and a lead ball (the bullet) down the barrel with a ramrod. He risked being shot by the enemy while he did this.

Bolt and firing mechanism

Rear sight

Blade sight

Steel barrel

Wooden stock

Trigger fires gun

Breech-loading rifle

🔔 BREECH-LOADERS

Breech-loading guns were loaded from the breech (rear) end of the barrel. The needle gun was a breech-loading rifle invented in 1837.

A cartridge contained the bullet, explosive and detonator. It could be fired and reloaded while lying down, so soldiers were in less danger from enemy fire.

Johannes von Dreyse, inventor of the needle gun

French troops fire Chassepot rifles in the Franco-Prussian War

🔔 CIVIL WAR RIFLES

In the USA, breech-loading rifles were used by both sides during the US Civil War. They were made by companies such as Hall, Joslyn and Jenks.

🔔 A BETTER WEAPON

The French made a breech-loading rifle called the Chassepot in 1866. It was much better than the Prussian needle gun. During the Franco-Prussian War, the Prussian army used Chassepots taken from captured or dead French infantrymen.

ARTILLERY

"Artillery" means "cannons and big mounted guns".

In the nineteenth century, some artillery was light enough to be mounted on gun carriages. These were pushed or pulled into position by one or two soldiers. Heavier guns were pulled by horses.

The Dictator

HUGE GUNS

Some big guns were so gigantic that they had to be mounted on railway wagons. One of these was the Dictator. This was a mortar (artillery that fired a shell) and it was used by the Union army during the US Civil War.

LOADING AND FIRING A CANNON

Ready...
A cloth bag of gunpowder and a cannon ball was rammed down the barrel of the gun.

Aim...
The gunner aimed the gun, poured the gunpowder charge into the touchhole and lit it.

Fire!
The gunpowder in the gun barrel exploded and the cannon ball flew towards the enemy.

AMMUNITION

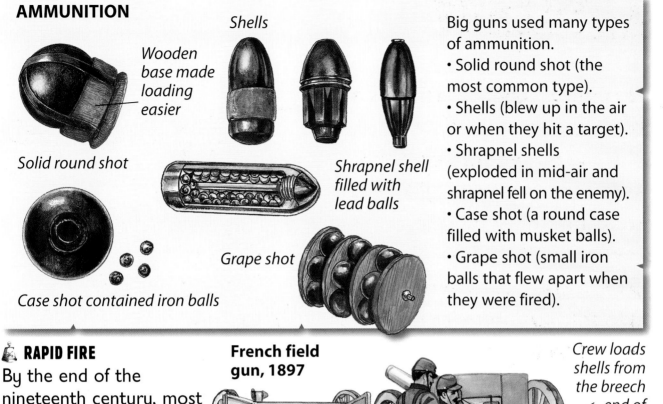

Solid round shot

Wooden base made loading easier

Shells

Solid round shot

Shrapnel shell filled with lead balls

Grape shot

Case shot contained iron balls

Big guns used many types of ammunition.
• Solid round shot (the most common type).
• Shells (blew up in the air or when they hit a target).
• Shrapnel shells (exploded in mid-air and shrapnel fell on the enemy).
• Case shot (a round case filled with musket balls).
• Grape shot (small iron balls that flew apart when they were fired).

🔥 RAPID FIRE

By the end of the nineteenth century, most armies had artillery that could be loaded from the breech end and which fired quickly. The French had a field gun that could fire twenty rounds per minute.

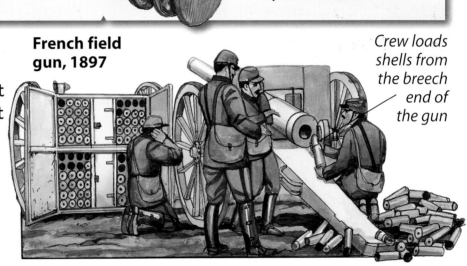

French field gun, 1897

Crew loads shells from the breech end of the gun

🔥 THE GUNNERS

Many guns were pulled by horses. But gunners also had to be strong enough to move them.

Each time the gun was fired, it moved. The gunners had to push and pull the gun back into position and aim it again.

An 1870s Prussian gun crew aims a field gun

ON THE MOVE

In the early 1800s, armies often marched thousands of miles to battle. As the century went on, the network of railways grew and trains became important for moving troops around in war.

British troops went to the Crimea and India by ship.

FRANCO-PRUSSIAN WAR

The French were not very good at using railways to move troops. But the Prussian army made good use of trains and this helped it to win the war.

A French troop train

SAILING TO INDIA

The only way to get soldiers to India was by ship. It took two months and conditions were bad. Many men died on the way and were buried at sea.

AMERICAN RAILWAYS

There were more railways in the northern states than in the south. This helped the Union army to move men and artillery to where they were needed.

But the Confederate army used trains too, where it could.

STEALING THE GENERAL

Union soldiers stole a Confederate steam locomotive, the *General*. They drove it until it ran out of steam and they were captured by the Confederates. The soldiers were executed (killed).

The *General*

ARMOURED MONSTER

New inventions made use of railways for war. The rail car below was used in the US Civil War. It had a cannon and armour plating to protect the crew.

Steam trains

Steam trains were made up of a locomotive (engine) and some carriages.

The locomotive burned coal to make the steam that powered it.

Steam trains at this time could travel at speeds of up to 90 km/h.

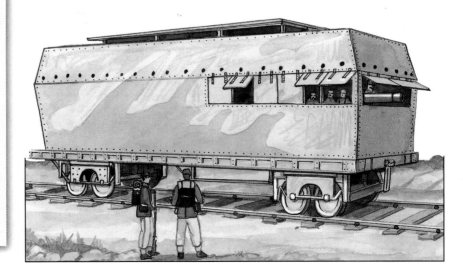

CAVALRY

The cavalry was made up of soldiers who rode horses. They helped to protect the infantry and artillery. Sometimes they charged at the enemy. At the end of a battle, they chased enemy soldiers who were running away. The cavalry was also used for reconnaissance – finding out what the enemy was doing.

Lord Raglan, commander-in-chief of the British army in the Crimea

THE LIGHT BRIGADE

In the Crimean War, the British Light Brigade (cavalry) was ordered to attack Russian guns at the Battle of Balaclava. The troops charged at the enemy but had to turn back. Nearly 250 men were killed or injured.

The Light Brigade charges at Balaclava

CAVALRYMAN'S KIT

Pistols and sabres

Cavalry troopers carried lots of equipment. They had weapons such as pistols and long swords called sabres.

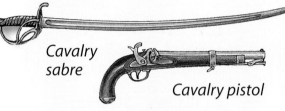

Cavalry sabre

Cavalry pistol

Officer's revolver

Saddlebags

Saddlebags were used to store a grooming kit for the horse, pen and paper, books and other personal items.

Blanket roll and canteen

Troopers had a blanket roll for sleeping and water in a canteen. They often carried a greatcoat to keep warm.

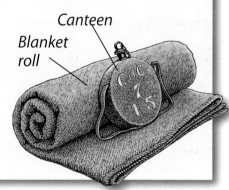

Canteen

Blanket roll

🔔 CHARGE!

To start a cavalry charge, the troops moved forward slowly. When they were about 700 metres from enemy lines, they started to trot. Just 180 metres from the enemy, they dashed forward in a charge.

Cavalry regiments
There were three types of troops in a cavalry regiment – assault, support and reserve.

In battle, assault and support troops moved forwards and broke into a trot. Then the assault troops made the charge.

🔔 CAVALRY IN THE US CIVIL WAR

Both sides had a large number of cavalrymen, but there were not many cavalry battles. Commanders mainly used horsemen for reconnaissance and for manoeuvres (army exercises) that were set up to confuse the enemy.

A Union cavalry trooper of the US Civil War

LIFE IN CAMP

In the Crimean War, there were only three major battles – Alma, Balaclava and Inkerman. But in the US Civil War, there were more than 230 battles.

When soldiers were not fighting, they lived in a camp. They spent their time eating, playing cards or simply waiting for the battle to start.

🔔 DRILLING

All soldiers had to do drill (practise manoeuvres). This helped to make them work well as a team and kept them ready to fight.

Prussian soldier drilling

🔔 OFF DUTY

Soldiers played games, read books and wrote letters home. Sometimes their families lived with them in camp.

A Union soldier and family at Camp Slocum, near Washington DC, in 1862

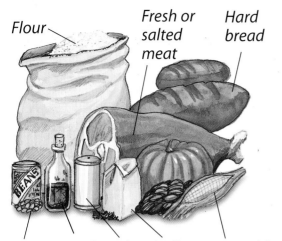

Flour

Fresh or salted meat

Hard bread

Beans Drink Salt Coffee Vegetables

A soldier's day

5.00 a.m. Drummer or bugler wakes everyone. Wash and dress.

5.15 a.m. Roll call.

5.30 a.m. Breakfast.

6.00 a.m. Chop firewood, clean camp and other duties.

8.00 a.m. Guard duty and drilling.

12 p.m. Dinner.

2.00 p.m. Drilling.

4.30 p.m. Get ready for evening inspection.

5.45 p.m. Roll call, inspection and parade.

6.30 p.m. Supper.

8.30 p.m. Last roll call.

9 p.m. Lights out.

🔔 FOOD

This picture shows the rations that a Union soldier was given each week. It was much better than the food of British soldiers in the Crimea — their usual meal was a thin stew of beef and potatoes.

Union soldiers raid a farm for pigs and chickens

🔔 LIVING OFF THE LAND

Soldiers tried to find other things to eat when they could. Some hunted wild animals and birds. Others stole chickens and pigs from farms.

• **Rations**
Each soldier was given a certain amount of food each day or week. This was called his rations.

• **Inspections and parades**
Soldiers' appearance and equipment were checked at inspections and parades (marches).

WAR AT SEA

In the nineteenth century, the British navy was the strongest in the world. Prussia and France were more interested in building up their armies than their navies. So, in Europe, navies did not have much to do in 1850–80. But in the US Civil War, there was a lot of fighting at sea.

Britain's first ironclad: HMS *Warrior*, 1860

🔔 IRONCLAD WARSHIPS

Ironclad ships were very strong. They had iron plating to protect them. The first ones were the French *La Gloire* of 1859, and the British HMS *Warrior* of 1860.

🔔 IRONCLADS IN THE USA

In the US Civil War, Confederate forces captured a Union ship, the USS *Merrimack*. They covered it with iron plating and renamed it the CSS *Virginia*. They also fitted an iron ram and ten cannons.

The crew of an ironclad on deck during the US Civil War

⚓ BATTLE OF THE IRONCLADS

The citizens of Washington DC (part of the Union) heard that the Confederate navy had the CSS *Virginia*, an iron warship. They were frightened that it would shell their city. So the US navy built an ironclad of its own, the USS *Monitor*. The two ships went into battle in March 1862.

⚓ FOUR-HOUR FIGHT

The *Virginia* and the *Monitor* fired their big guns at each other for four hours. Then the ships' commanders decided to call it a draw and sailed off.

The battle between the *Monitor* and the *Virginia* in 1862

CSS Virginia

USS Monitor

Ironclads
• *"Ironclad" means "clad (covered) in iron".*

• *Iron is a metal that is often used for engineering (making engines, machines and bridges).*

• *HMS Warrior, the first British ironclad warship, never did any fighting. It can be seen today at the Historic Dockyard, Portsmouth, UK.*

⚓ THE MONITOR'S TURRET

The *Monitor* was armed with two huge cannons. These were in an armoured turret that turned round so the guns could be fired in any direction.

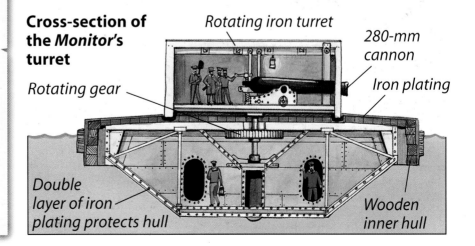

Cross-section of the *Monitor's* turret

Rotating iron turret

280-mm cannon

Iron plating

Rotating gear

Double layer of iron plating protects hull

Wooden inner hull

MEDICINE

More soldiers died of illnesses and infections than from being killed in battle. Military hospitals were filthy.

In the Crimean War, conditions started to get better when nurses such as Florence Nightingale and Mary Seacole went to the Crimea. By the end of the nineteenth century, medical care had improved a lot.

FLORENCE NIGHTINGALE
Florence Nightingale (above) went to the Crimea to nurse injured soldiers. She was horrified by the dirty conditions she found. She and her nurses worked very hard and death rates started to fall.

HOSPITALS
Conditions in military field hospitals were dreadful. Surgeons used dirty, bloodstained instruments. Anaesthetics (a way of stopping a patient feeling pain during an operation) were hardly ever used. Men who survived the operations often died later from fever.

A US Civil War military hospital

SURGEON'S KIT, 1850s

Army surgeons (doctors who did operations) had instruments for different types of injury. There were knives to cut through flesh, saws to cut bone, probes and bullet extractors to find and pull out bullets.

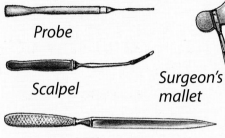

Bone saw

Surgical saw

Probe

Scalpel

Amputation knife

Surgeon's mallet

Tools to bore into bone

Bone crimper

Bullet extractor

Bone cutter

Henri Dunant with the flag of the Red Cross

🔔 THE RED CROSS

A Swiss man called Henri Dunant saw how soldiers suffered in war.

In 1862 he published a leaflet saying that a group was needed to care for wounded soldiers in wartime. The Red Cross started because of this.

🔔 LUCKY LOCALS

The British army in India had Indian soldiers called sepoys in it. They did not catch many of the illnesses that killed the British soldiers.

Indian sepoy of the 41st Regiment Bengal Native Infantry

Amputations
Sometimes soldiers had to have a badly injured arm or leg amputated (cut off). This was often done without an anaesthetic. Many died afterwards from infections because the hospitals were so dirty and full of germs. Little was known about germs at the time.

WAR NEWS

The fastest way to send news and messages was by telegraph. The sender used a machine to send pulses of electric current along telegraph wires. The pulses arrived at the other end as a pattern of dots and dashes. Telegraph operators could work out the message from the pattern.

People in Britain read about the Crimean War in *The Times*

Confederate troops lay a telegraph wire

📷 WAR REPORTER
During the Crimean War, *The Times* newspaper sent a journalist called William Howard Russell to the Crimea. He was the first proper war reporter.

📷 TELEGRAPH WIRES
At first there were not many telegraph stations and telegraph wires. But they soon spread across many countries.

By the US Civil War, there was a wide network of telegraph wires in the USA.

CRIMEAN HORROR

In the Crimea, Russell did not just write about who won the battles. His reports in *The Times* described the awful conditions that the soldiers faced.

A report from Russell:
"The men suffered exceedingly from cold. Some of them had no beds to lie on and none had more than their single regulation blanket. They dressed to go to bed, putting on all their spare clothing before they tried to sleep."

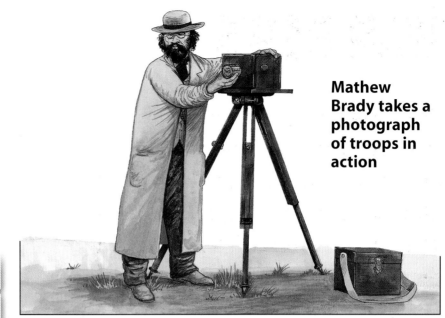

Mathew Brady takes a photograph of troops in action

PHOTOGRAPHING THE ACTION

During the US Civil War, a photographer called Mathew Brady was allowed to photograph army units. By the end of the war, he had taken more than 3,500 photographs. These showed civilians how horrible war was.

Photograph of Union troops by Mathew Brady, 1864

GLOSSARY

Artillery
The large guns (cannons and mounted guns) of an army and the men who use them.

The Balkans
The large peninsula in south-east Europe, between the Adriatic and Aegean Seas.

Bolt
A sliding bar in a breech-loading gun.

Union general

It ejects a used cartridge and guides a new one into the breech.

British East India Company
The company that ran India for the British government until just after the Indian Mutiny.

Cavalry
Soldiers on horseback.

c. (circa)
A Latin word meaning "about". It is used with a date to show that historians are not sure of the exact date.

Civilian
Non-military.

Confederate states
The southern states of the USA that broke away from the others in 1860, starting the US Civil War.

Conscription/ conscript
Compulsory military service (often, but not always, in wartime).

Crimea
A peninsula in Russia between the Black Sea and the Sea of Azov.

Empire
Group of states, countries or territories that were once independent (not controlled by another country or power), but now ruled by a single country or person.

Fusilier
A private in a British rifle regiment.

Guardsman
A private in a British Guards regiment.

Gunner
A private in Britain's Royal Regiment of Artillery.

Grape shot
Cannon ammunition made of small iron balls that scatter after firing.

Infantry
The foot soldiers of an army.

Kepi
A military cap with a circular top and a horizontal peak.

Manoeuvres
Military exercises for soldiers to practise what they have learned.

Military
Something that is to do with the armed forces.

Militiamen
Civilians who volunteer for military training so they can become a home defence force and increase army numbers in war.

Musket
A muzzle-loading shoulder gun used from c. 1650 to the mid-1800s.

Mutiny
A rebellion against authority (resisting it, rising up against it or fighting it).

Officer
A soldier above the rank of regimental sergeant-major.

Private
The lowest rank in any army.

Prussia
The most powerful German state in the nineteenth century. It wanted to make all independent German states into one country.

Ramrod
A rod used to push ammunition into the barrel of a gun.

Regiment
A large military unit, usually made up of battalions and often divided into companies and platoons.

Roll call
A register taken to check who is present.

Sabre
A long, curved, single-edged sword for use on horseback.

Shako
A peaked cap, also known as a "stovepipe", worn by soldiers of many countries throughout the nineteenth century until the introduction of the helmet (in Britain, around 1878).

Shell
Hollow artillery ammunition. It was

British soldier loading his musket

filled with explosives that exploded during flight or when it hit its target. It could also be filled with pieces of shrapnel.

Shrapnel
Small pellets or bullets in a shell, which explode before it lands. Or fragments from a shell.

State
An area with its own government.

Telegraph
Electric signals sent along a transmission wire. Used to send information.

Union states
The northern states in the US Civil War. They fought the Confederates (southern states).

INDEX

PHOTOGRAPHIC CREDITS

Peter Newark's American Pictures pp. 22, 29
Peter Newark's Military Pictures pp. 10, 17, 24, 26